Yak-130

Advanced Trainer/Light Combat Aircraft

HUGH HARKINS

Copyright © 2019 Hugh Harkins

All rights reserved.

ISBN: 1-903630-89-4
ISBN-13: 978-1-903630-89-1

Yak-130

Advanced Trainer/Light Combat Aircraft

© Hugh Harkins 2019

Centurion Publishing
United Kingdom

ISBN 10: 1-903630-89-4
ISBN 13: 978-1-903630-89-1

This volume first published in 2019

The Author is identified as the copyright holder of this work under sections 77 and 78 of the Copyright Designs and Patents Act 1988

Cover design © Centurion Publishing and KDP
Page layout, concept and design © Centurion Publishing

All rights reserved. No part of this publication may be reproduced, stored in a retrieval system, transmitted in any form, or by any means, electronic, mechanical or photocopied, recorded or otherwise, without the written permission of the publisher

The publisher and author would like to thank all organisations and services for their assistance and contributions in the preparation of this volume: Central Aerodynamic Institute; China National Aero-Technology Import & Export Corporation; FSUE MMPP Salut; GosMKB Vympel; JSC A.S. Yakovlev Design Bureau; JSC Aviaavtomatika; JSC Experimental Design Bureau Electroautomatics; JSC Irkut Corporation (Irkutsk Aviation Plant); JSC Tactical Missiles Corporation; Ministry of Defence of the Russian Federation; Ministry of Defence of the Republic of Belarus; Moscow Institute of Electromechanics and Automatics; PJSC Sukhoi Company; PJSC UEC Saturn; Rosoboronexport; Rostec Corporation; Russian Aircraft Corporation; SE Ivchenko-Progress; Scientific-Production Enterprise Zvezda & United Aircraft Corporation

Citation guide: (TsAGI) Central Aerodynamic Institute; (CATIC) China National Aero-Technology Import & Export Corporation; (Salut) FSUE MMPP Salut; (Vympel) GosMKB Vympel; (Yakovlev) JSC A.S. Yakovlev Design Bureau; (Aviaavtomatika) JSC Aviaavtomatika; (Electroautomatics) JSC Experimental Design Bureau Electroautomatics; (Irkut) JSC Irkut Corporation (Irkutsk Aviation Plant); (TMC) JSC Tactical Missiles Corporation; (MODRF) Ministry of Defence of the Russian Federation; (MODRB) Ministry of Defence of the Republic of Belarus; (MIEA) Moscow Institute of Electromechanics and Automatics; (Sukhoi) PJSC Sukhoi Company; (UEC Saturn) PJSC UEC Saturn; (Rosoboronexport) Rosoboronexport; (Rostec) Rostec Corporation; (RAC) Russian Aircraft Corporation; (Ivchenko-Progress) SE Ivchenko-Progress; (Zvezda) Scientific-Production Enterprise Zvezda & (UAC) United Aircraft Corporation

CONTENTS

	Introduction	vii
1	Yak-130 Short Genesis/History	1
2	Yak-130 – Advanced Trainer/Light Combat Aircraft	9
3	Glossary	73

INTRODUCTION

The Yak-130 entered service with the Russian Federation Air Force (Aerospace Forces from August 2015) in 2010, as a new generation training system for basic and advanced pilot training with a secondary light combat aircraft role.
The intent of this volume is to detail the Yak-130 from s systems point of view with only a brief genesis/historic overview. All technical information regarding the aircraft, systems and weapons have been provided by the respective design houses/developers and experimental agencies, as has most of the graphic material, with technical and graphic input from other entities, such as the Ministry of Defence of the Russian Federation and Ministry of Defence of the Republic of Belarus – the later nation operating the Yak-130 as a light combat aircraft.

1

YAK-130 SHORT GENESIS/HISTORY

The Yak-130 was designed and developed as an advanced training aircraft capable of replicating the characteristics of contemporary combat aircraft, and also be capable of conducting a secondary LCA (Light Combat Aircraft) mission armed with precision guided and unguided air to air and air to surface weapons. In the primary role of advanced flight trainer, the Yak-130, allocated the NATO (North Atlantic Treaty Organisation) reporting name 'Mitten', is intended for the training of pilots progressing to $4^{th}+$, $4^{th}++$ and 5th generation combat aircraft – including the $4^{th}+$ generation Sukhoi Su-34 multifunctional strike aircraft, $4^{th}+$ generation RAC MiG MiG-29KR/KUBR fleet multifunctional strike fighter, $4^{th}+$ generation Sukhoi Su-30SM multifunctional strike fighter, $4^{th}++$ generation Sukhoi Su-35S and RAC MiG MiG-35/D multidimensional strike fighters and the 5th generation Sukhoi Su-57 multidimensional strike fighter (UAC).

Development of the aircraft design recognisable as the serial Yak-130 had commenced at A.S. Yakovlev Design Bureau in the early 1990's, with the aim of arriving at a design to replace the USSR (Union of Soviet Socialist Republics) fleet of subsonic Aero L-39 advanced jet trainer aircraft (UAC). Initial planning, formulated in 1991, called for deliveries of trials examples of the new training aircraft design to the Soviet Defence Ministry in 1995 – the USSR (Soviet Union) was dissolved into a Commonwealth of Independent States on 25 December 1991, the new advanced training aircraft thereafter being developed for the Russian Federation. Yakovlev had a legacy of experience on turbojet powered combat aircraft development, and limited experience in advanced jet trainer aircraft design and development. The design house had, in completion with the Polish TS-11 and Czechoslovak L-29 advanced jet trainer aircraft designs, developed the Yak-30 as an advanced jet trainer for the Soviet Air Forces in the 1950's. The L-29 was selected for serial production and the Yak-30 fell by the wayside, as did the Yak-30 derived Yak-32. The Soviet Air Forces selected the Czechoslovak Aero L-39 to replace the L-29, the L-39 remaining in service in 2019, alongside the Yak-130, with the Russian Federation Aerospace Forces and Naval Aviation training units (MODRF).

The Yak-130 entered Russian Air Force service in 2010 as the reorganisation and re-equipment of that service began to ramp up as funds were increasingly allocated for modernisation. UAC

The L-39 was a capable aircraft for training pilots preparing to move forward to 4th generation combat aircraft such as the Mikoyan MiG-31 long-range interceptor, Sukhoi Su-25 ground attack aircraft, Mikoyan MiG-29 frontal fighter, Sukhoi Su-27 air superiority fighter and the aircraft carrier capable Sukhoi Su-27K (the Su-27K was adopted for service with Russian Naval Aviation as the Su-33 in 1998). However, with the advancements in combat aircraft and related systems design through the late 1980's and into the 1990's, it had become clear that a new advanced training aircraft would be required to adequately prepare pilots for moving onto the new generation of multifunctional aircraft under development – in the early 1990's this was typified by the Sukhoi Su-27M (this design, developed from the first generation Su-27S, was cancelled in the early 2000's as studies moved toward more advanced multidimensional strike fighter aircraft designs that emerged as the Su-35S and Su-57) and the first generation MiG-29M and naval MiG-29K (these designs fell by the wayside and MiG-29 development was focused on the Unified family of 4th+ generation MiG-29M (second generation), 4th+ generation MiG-29K/KR/KUB/KUBR (second generation) and 4th++ generation MiG-35/D). The new trainer aircraft was to be designed from the outset for training pilots progressing to what would be termed aircraft featuring 'super manoeuvrability'.

In 2019, the Aero L-39 remains in service as an advanced trainer aircraft in the Russian Federation Aerospace Forces (top) and Naval Aviation (above). MODRF/Ilyushin

Model of the Sukhoi S-54 advanced jet trainer/light combat aircraft design circa mid-1990's, shown at the Farnborough International Trade show in September 1996. Author

The basic design concept for the new advanced jet training aircraft, which would emerge as the Yak-130, was completed in 1993 and approved by the MODRF (Ministry of Defence of the Russian Federation) that year. The Yak-130 main rivals for the Russian Air Force advanced training aircraft requirement was the Mikoyan Design Bureau (later Russian Aircraft Corporation) MiG AT, with the Sukhoi S-54 a ranked outsider. This latter design was oriented more toward the LCA role than was the Yakovlev and MiG designs. The 1996/1997 S-54/55 (the S-55 was a single crew derivative of the S-54, intended solely for the LCA role) variants adopted the canard tri-plane layout developed on a number of Su-27 variants. Although outwardly appearing to be a smaller Su-27 derivative, there were many differences in layout, not least of which was the single-engine design, air intake configuration and outwardly canted vertical tail fins. The power plant was centred on a single Lyulka (UEC Saturn) AL-31F afterburning turbofan engine rated at 79.43 kN (17,857 lb.) dry and 122.59 kN (27,558 lb.) with afterburner, whereas the Su-27S was powered by two such units (Sukhoi & UEC Saturn).

Projected performance values released by Sukhoi for the 1996 S-54 light combat aircraft variant (modified variant of the original S-54 advanced trainer submission) showed a maximum speed of 1200 km/h at sea level and 1650 km/h at upper altitude, with a ceiling of 18 km. The S-54/55 were designed for high agility with *g*-limit load factor values of +12/-3, and the design featured a projected operational range of 820 km and a 3000 km ferry range (Sukhoi). While agility and operating ceiling were better than competitors, range fell below that required. There was no Russian domestic interest in either the S-54 or S-55 and neither type was considered for further development, larger more capable aircraft like the Sukhoi Su-30 variants being more attractive to customers moving to 4+ generation combat aircraft over the ensuing two decades. The unbuilt S-54/55 designs slipped into obscurity, leaving the Yak-130 and MiG AT in a head to head to meet the Russian requirement for an advanced training aircraft with a secondary light combat aircraft capability.

The main rival to the Yak-130 in the competition to field a new generation advanced training aircraft for the Russian Air Force was the MiG AT. Development aircraft White 81 is taxiing at the Farnborough International Trade show in September 1996 (top) and Red 83 is taxiing at Le Bourget Paris in 2001 (bottom). Author

Mikoyan Design Bureau had commenced development of the MiG AT in the early 1990's, the demonstrator being built during 1995-1996 and flown in March of the latter year (RAC). This design, which adopted a low set conventional wing monoplane configuration with a single vertical tail and all-moving horizontal tail-planes, was powered by two AL-55 turbofan engines developed by Lyulka (UEC Saturn). The engines were mounted in fuselage engine bays either side of the fuselage at the blend into the wing-fuselage join section.

Page 6-7: Yak-130D demonstrator, RA-43130, at Le Bourget, Paris, in June 1997. Author

The Yak-130 was selected to proceed to full-scale development. However, the adverse economic conditions prevalent in the post-Soviet Russia of the 1990's translated to inadequate state funding for the program, resulting in Yakovlev entering into program cooperation with Aermacchi (now part of Leonardo company) of Italy. This cooperation, which commenced in 1993 and ended in 1999, resulted in a decision to proceed with construction of a demonstrator aircraft designated Yak-130D. This aircraft conducted its maiden flight from the airfield at Gromov on 25 April 1993 (pilot, Andrey Sinitsen (Yakovlev Design Bureau)). When the joint Russo/Italian program ended in 1999, Yakovlev continued development of the Yak-130, which was based on new technologies and the results of flight testing conducted with the Yak-130D demonstrator, which were instrumental in determining the design intended for serial production for the Russian Federation Air Force.

During the period 2000-2002, production documentation was prepared for the revised Yak-130 design. With its removal from the program to develop a future 5th generation fighter design for the Russian Federation Air Force, Yakovlev was effectively out of the fighter design and building business, but aimed to remain a viable combat aircraft design house with the Yak-130 advanced trainer/light combat aircraft design, which was announced as the winner of the Ministry of Defence of the Russian Federation advanced jet trainer competition on 16 April 2002. By this time the aircraft program was oriented toward provisioning a platform to meet the Russian Federations requirement for an intermediate/advanced jet trainer aircraft to train crew for Russia's new generation of $4^{th}+$, $4^{th}++$ and 5th generation aircraft then being prepared for service or planned for the second decade of the twenty first century.

Top: The Yak-130D takes-off on the first day of the 1997 Paris Air Salon, Le Bourget airport, June 1997. Above: At the end of the cooperation phase with Yakovlev, Aermacchi (now Leonardo) embarked upon the M-346 advanced trainer/light combat aircraft, which was based on the Yak-130 design. Author

2

YAK-130 – ADVANCED TRAINER/LIGHT COMBAT AIRCRAFT

Preproduction work on the serial Yak-130 design was conducted during 2003. Two development aircraft, to be built during 2003-2005, were ordered. The first of these development examples was completed at the Sokol Aviation Plant, located in Nizhny Novgorod, Russia, in December 2003. The aircraft was moved to Yakovlev's facility for a static test phase in January 2004. This phase involved various onboard equipment/systems testing, complementing equipment/systems testing conducted on test stands. The stand testing included demonstrations of the control system, conducted by Yakovlev, a series of bench testing of the power complex and ground based trials of the emergency escape system conducted on a high speed jet powered rail platform (UAC).

The maiden flight of the prototype development aircraft, allocated the code 01, was conducted from the Sokol Plant on 30 April 2004 (pilot, Yakovlev Design Bureau chief test pilot, Roman Taskaev). The second development aircraft, 02, conducted its maiden flight on 5 April 2005 (crew, test pilots Vasily Sevastyanov and Roman Taskaev) (UAC). A third development aircraft, Yak-130 03, was ordered. This aircraft was structurally complete in December 2005 and conducted its maiden flight on 27 March 2006 (pilots, Oleg Kononenko (Yakovlev Design Bureau) and Colonel Setgei Shcherbina (MODRF)). Following a further three flights, which completed the factory test phase, Yak-130 03 was transferred to the LII facility at Zhukovsky where it was integrated into the State Joint Test phase (UAC). To replace a development Yak-130 lost in an accident in 2006, a fourth development Yak-130 was ordered, to be procured through insurance funds paid for the destroyed aircraft. This aircraft was manufactured with hast and entered the overall test program in June 2009 (UAC).

Although there were certain nuanced changes, the serial Yak-130 design retained much of the Yak-130D aerodynamic layout and control, including the spine-mounted air-brake, but dispensed with certain design traits, such as the upward turned winglets at the wingtips. The basic design layout of the serial Yak-130 is that of a tandem cockpit mid-wing monoplane with moderate sweepback of the wing (Yakovlev), a single vertical tail fin and all-moving horizontal tail-planes. Control surfaces include the two-piece trailing edge ailerons (flaps), the two-piece leading edge flaps on each wing, all moving horizontal tail planes and the vertical tail-plane rudder that extends from the base of the vertical tail to roughly one sixth from the top. The other major control surface is the air-brake, which opens toward the forward hemisphere from its position on the aircraft spine, just forward of the base of the vertical tail. The basic dimensions for the Yak-130 serial design include a length of 11.49 m, height, 4.76 m, wingspan, 9.72 m (9.84 m with wingtip stores) and wing area, 23.52 m^2 (Irkut). The wing is designed to sustain subsonic flight at varying angles of attack up to 35-40°, allowing the aircraft to emulate the outstanding flight characteristics of the new generation of 'super maneuverable' fighter designs (Irkut), such as the Sukhoi Su-35S, Su-30SM and Su-57.

Previous page: Russian Federation Aerospace Forces Yak-130, 27 June 2019 (top) and a model of the Yak-130 tested at TsAGI (Central Aerodynamic Institute) at high angle-of-attack and corkscrew flight regimes (bottom). This page: The prototype Yak-130 in the assembly hall at Sokol Aviation Plant (top) and a Yak-130 airframe undergoing fatigue/endurance tests at the Central Aerodynamic Institute. UAC/TsAGI

Top: The Yak-130 was put through an extensive airframe endurance/fatigue test regime at the Central Aerodynamic Institute. **Above:** The Aermacchi M-346 adopted the basic Yak-130 layout, albeit with some major and nuanced changes. TsAGI/Leonardo

The basic Yak-130 design formed the basis of the Aermacchi M-346 advanced jet trainer. Whilst there are many nuanced design changes along with several major changes, the M-346 is unmistakably derived from the Yak-130 design, retaining the same basic dimensions of length, height and wingspan associated with the Yak-130 – 11.49 m, 4.76 m and 9.72 m respectively (Leonardo). The M-346 also adopted a similar spin-mounted airbrake (repositioned), similar air intakes and cockpit canopy opening. It is internally that both designs differ most, the Italian aircraft adopting an American power plant in the shape of the Honeywell F-124 and the avionics systems sourced from western nation suppliers.

Extract from UAC Russian language Yak-130 infographic that basically translates to refer to aircraft type, designer and primary role –to train crew for 4th and 5th generation combat aircraft, which can be replicated in subsonic flight regimes –and provides some basic design details: engine type, number, power output; refers to the three 6 x 8 displays (in each cockpit) and basic dimensions of length, 11.483 m; height, 4.76 m; wingspan, 9.84 m (with wingtip stores) and wing area, 23.52 m².

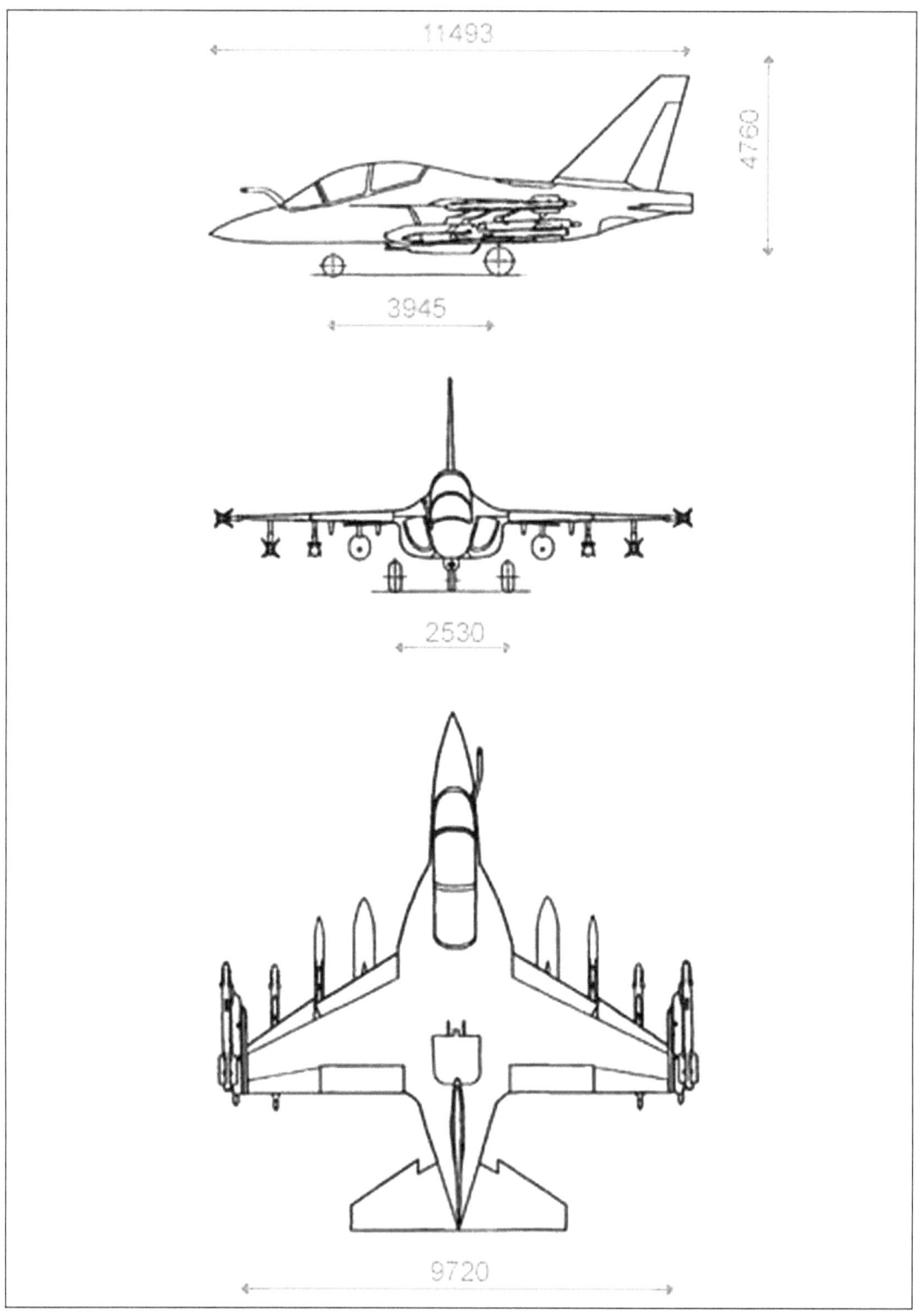

Three-view general arrangement drawing of the Yak-130 with a non-standard fixed in-flight refueling probe. Basic dimensions are in mm. Yakovlev/UAC

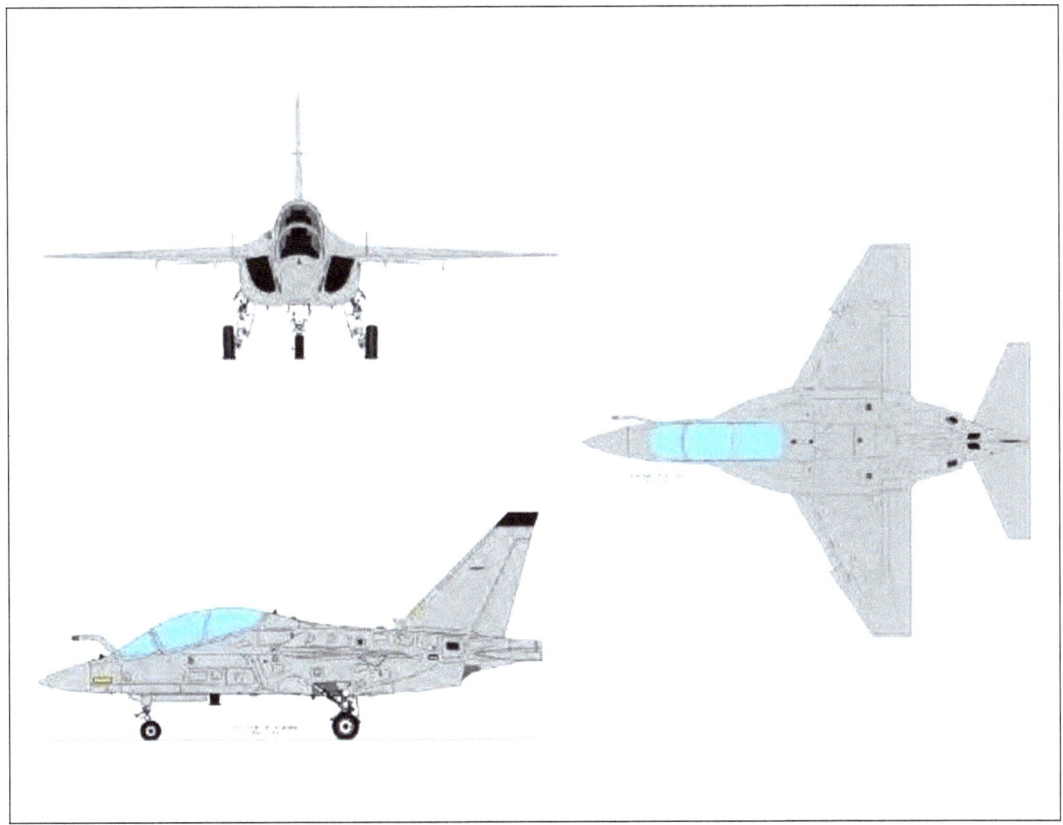

Three-view general arrangement drawing of the Aermacchi (Leonardo) M-346, showing the clear Yak-130 design lineage. Leonardo

The Central Aerodynamic Institute (TsAGI)) conducted research into the fatigue life of the Yak-130 airframe, which included extensive endurance tests conducted on a specially constructed stand configured for 'modelling of aerodynamic and inertial forces on all airframe units, wing with mechanization, fuselage, horizontal and vertical tail, engine mount and chassis assemblies' – testing relating to ground and flight operations in various flight regimes and load conditions for the latter (TsAGI).

The Yak-130 possesses a high degree of maneuverability, excellent take-off, landing and flight handling qualities at low speeds and good climb rate (TsAGI). As well as the traditional conventional control surfaces, the Yak-130 is equipped with a complex of air intake shields on the forward fuselage upper surfaces above both engine intakes in the forward section of the engine bay trunks. This, among other work on the Yak-130 aerodynamic layout, was a major area of design participation for TsAGI. The air intakes were designed for high operational efficiency of the engines when at various high angles of attack flight regimes. The intake-guards can be activated during ground operation to avoid foreign object ingestion – an intake guard blocking the main intake – and during certain flight regimes, such as when the aircraft is in the landing pattern. This contributes to an increment in aircraft safety in the event of foreign objects in the flight path.

Yak-130 development aircraft White 01. Irkut

Yak-130 development aircraft White 02. Irkut

Air intakes with shields

Previous page top: Still graphic showing the layout of the Yak-130 air intake system, incorporating foreign object ingestion shields. Previous page bottom: Yak-130 in flight with the upper fuselage intake doors open. This page: Yak-130 in flight with upper fuselage intake doors closed (top) and with intake shields deployed (bottom). UAC/Ivchenko-Progress /Irkut/MODRF

The Yak-130 was designed with a lever-type tricycle landing gear incorporating low pressure tyres. UAC/Irkut

Yak-130's White 02 (top) and White 01 (bottom) in the landing pattern with undercarriage deployed. UAC/Yakovlev

The air intake guards contribute to the Yak-130 excellent unpaved field capability that is further enabled by the robust undercarriage design. The undercarriage is a relatively conventional tricycle type lever style design, incorporating low pressure tyres with single wheel main units that retract into the engine bay trunks and a single nose wheel unit that retracts aft to be housed in the forward fuselage underside, beneath the forward cockpit section.

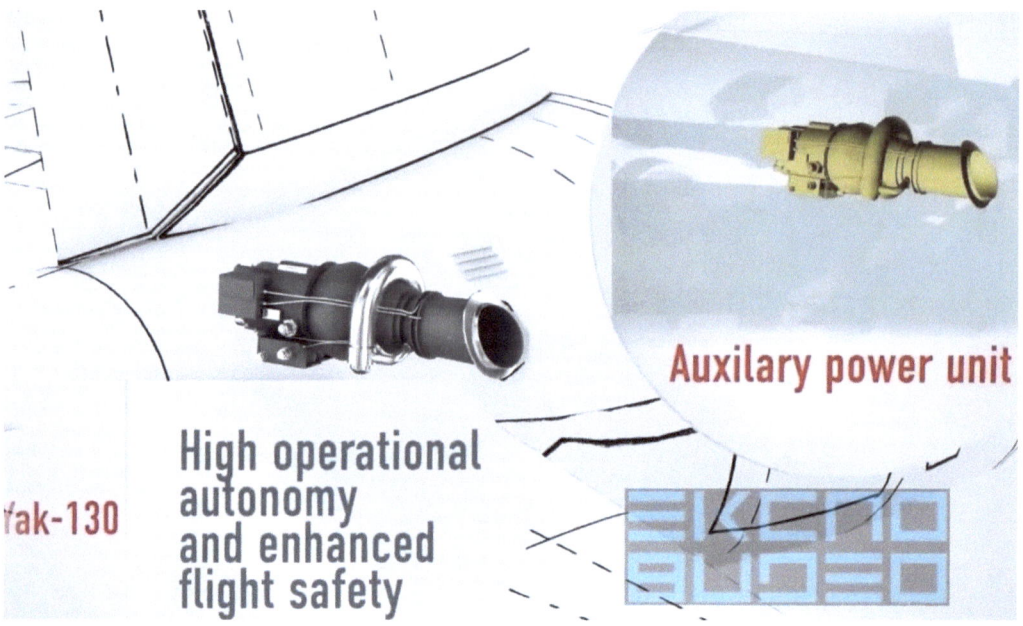

Graphic depicting the layout and position of the TA 14-130 auxiliary power unit installation in the Yak-130. UAC

The air intake debris guards and lever type landing gear design, combined with the incorporation of a TA 14-130 APU (Auxiliary Power Unit) contribute to the Yak-130 high operational autonomy and enhanced ground and flight safety design features. This facilitates the Yak-130 ability to operate from unpaved airfields, a good quality for an aircraft that has a secondary LCA (Light Combat Aircraft) role for battlefield support operations, whereby the design may be forward deployed not too far from the area of operations. The APU, with alternating current, can be employed during ground operations and during an inflight emergency, such as an engine restart. (Irkut).

The Yak-130 is powered by two Ivchenko-Progress AI-222-25 non-afterburning turbofan engines, each of which can develop a maximum thrust rating of 2200 kg. The engines generate a thrust to weight ratio in the order of 0.81, bestowing upon the Yak-130 excellent flight performance in many areas, such as speed, acceleration, climb, and also take-off performance (Irkut), for an aircraft in its class. The AI-222-25 engine (also referred to under the RD-35 designation by the MODRF), which received state certification at the completion of tests in 2005 (UAC), incorporates a two-stage low pressure compressor, Blisk technology – the blades are manufactured as an integral element of the compressor disk in the production process. Other major elements of the design include an '8-stage high pressure compressor, an annular combustion chamber, a single stage LP (Low Pressure) turbine and a single-stage HP (High Pressure) turbine, and a nozzle [engine exhaust]' (Rosoboronexport). The accessory gearbox section is located on the engine underside.

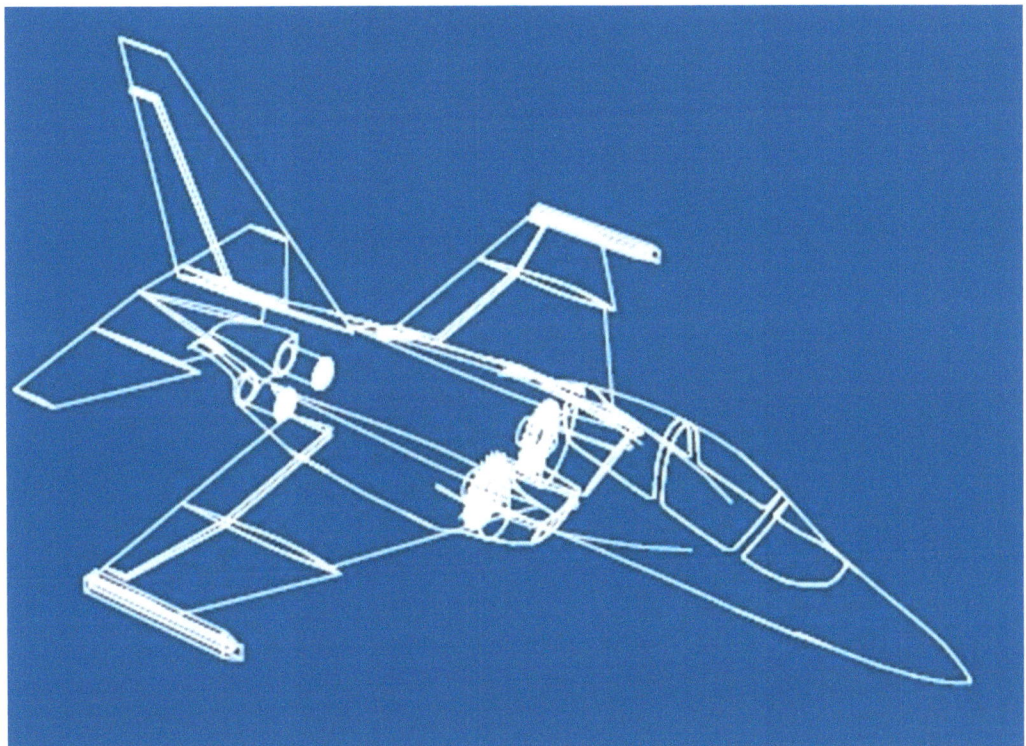

Top: AI-222-25 turbofan engine. Above: Ghosted diagram of the Yak-130 showing the side-by-side layout of the engines and bays Ivchenko-Progress /UAC

Top: Yak-130 White 02 performing a roll, revealing the external layout of the engine bays on the fuselage sides/undersides. Above: Line-up of Yak-130's of the Russian Aerospace Forces showing the exhaust nozzle and nozzle bays on the rear fuselage underside. Irkut/Rostec

Yak-130 White 01 banks to port revealing the engine exhaust channel on the rear fuselage underside. Yakovlev

The AI-222-25, and the AI-222-28 derivative, can be equipped with a thrust-vector control system, although this is not installed on the engine powering the serial production Yak-130 (Salut). Another AI-222-25 derivative is the AI-322, featuring augmented thrust (afterburner), which powers the Chinese CATIC L-15 AJT and the notional Yak-135 LCA development of the Yak-130 (Ivchenko-Progress).

The AI-225-25 development program was completed in 2009 and acceptance of the results of Joint State Tests was signed with the Russian Defence Ministry that year. Serial production of the AI-222-25 is conducted in cooperation between JSC Motor Sich (through UkOboronProm) and FSUE Salut MMPP (Ivchenko-Progress & Salut).

AI-222-25 – Ivchenko-Progress /FSUE Salut MMPP/Rosoboronexport

Length: 2238 mm
Fan diameter: 624 mm
Inlet dimeter: 634 mm
Weight dry: 440 kg +2%
Maximum power conditions (SLS, ISA, Yin=1.0)
Maximum thrust: 2500 kgf (24.52 kN) flat rated to t_{AMB} =+30° Centigrade (4500 kgf with afterburner for AI-2225F (AI-332/F))– not available on the Yak-130
Specific fuel consumption: 0.64+2% kg/kgf/h (MMPP Salut states 0.63 kg/kgf/h)
Maximum power conditions: Hn= 5000 m; Mn= 0.6; ISA; Yin= 0.97)
Thrust: 1450 kgf (14.22 kN)
By-pass ratio: 1.18
Air consumption: 49.4 kg/s
Pressurisation ratio: 15.4
Maximum gas temperature before the turbine: 1471 Kelvin

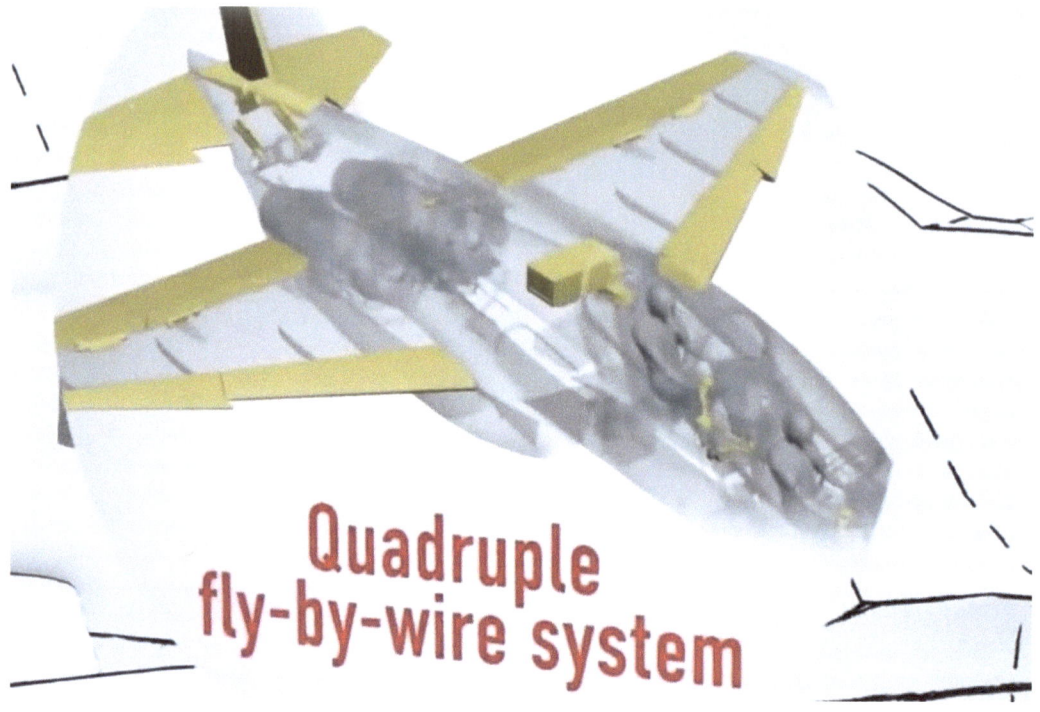

Diagram showing the central location within the Yak-130 of the KSU-130 quadruple redundant digital fly-by-wire flight control system and some of the surfaces controlled. UAC

The Yak-130 was to be designed from the outset to be capable of emulating the performance characteristics of $4^{th}+$, $4^{th}++$ and 5th generation tactical combat aircraft in flight regimes at subsonic speeds. The main driver for this outstanding performance capability is the incorporation of an advanced digital FBW (Fly-By-Wire) FCS (Flight Control System) in combination with airframe and engine designs (UAC). The KSU-130 integrated flight control system, developed for the Yak-130, is a quadruple redundant unit with 70 channels. The FBW FCS incorporates an 'active flight safety capability and a reprogrammable capability that makes it possible to modify the stability and controllability characteristics of the aircraft' (Rosoboronexport). This allows it to fulfil the requirement of emulating the flight characteristics of other aircraft. The complex is made up of the following components – К-56, ДПР-3 (DPR-3), ДАП-3-1 (DAP-3-1), БДГ-30-1 (BDG-30-1), ДАУ-19 (DAU-19), МВД-Д1 (MVD-D1), П-104 (P-104) hydraulic actuators. The FCS provides for remote operation of the following: 'manual wheel control through electrohydraulic actuators; manual and automatic leading-edges control; manual and automatic trailing-edges control' (MIEA). The system also provides 'automatic and director control, calculation and release of information on marginal flight configurations' and 'calculation and release altitude-velocity parameters' (MIEA). The complex detects, saves and stores data regarding faults in the onboard computer control system (Irkut).

The KSU-130 fly-by-wire flight control system provisions for the Yak-130 flight capabilities in all flight modes, as well as various ground operations. Irkut

Previous page: The Yak-130 two crew are seated in tandem. This page: As was the case with the Yak-130D, the serial Yak-130 cockpit canopy hinges open to starboard. Irkut

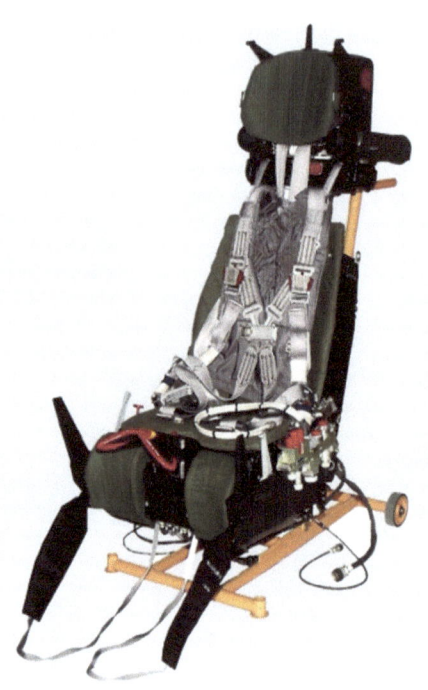

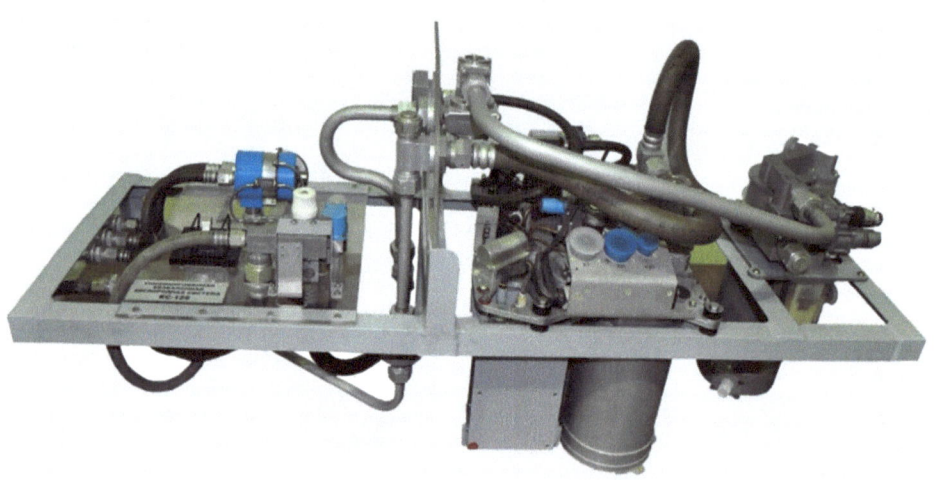

Top: K-36L-3.5YA zero-zero ejection seat equipping both cockpits of the Yak-130. Above: The Yak-130 is equipped with a KS-130 oxygen system designed to supply the crew with oxygen at flight altitudes up to 12 km. Zvezda

The serial Yak-130 is equipped with K-36L-3.5YA zero-zero ejection seats in both cockpits. These units are lightweight modifications of the K-36D-3.5 employed on tactical combat aircraft such as the Su-30SM – the K-36L-3.5YA has an installation weight of 86 kg. The ejection-seats, which are part of the overall EES (Emergency Escape System), catapult the occupant away from the aircraft in the event of an irrecoverable emergency – the ejection sequence commences with the destruction of the cockpit canopy through piorshnurom (pyrotechnic charge shattering of the canopy) (Irkut). Once free of the aircraft the pilot separates from the seat and the descent parachute deploys. The emergency escape module also incorporates a portable emergency reserve location beacon, which is activated once on the surface. If the landing occurs on water then the crew can deploy PSN-1 rafts to support them in the water until rescue arrives (Zvezda). The ejection-seat is designed for activation at flight velocity ranging from 0 to 1050 km/h at flight altitudes of 0 to 13000 m (in excess of the Yak-130 operating ceiling). It is capable of effective operation when the aircraft is at 0 altitude and 0 airspeed (Zvezda).

The EES is equipped with a KKO-15 oxygen system, complementing the KS-130 oxygen system, which supplies the crew with oxygen at flight altitudes up to 12 km via a BKDU-130 onboard oxygen producing unit. This unit produces oxygen from compressed air that has been taken from the aircraft engine compressor, removing the requirement for accommodating onboard oxygen cylinders, which have to be recharged prior to flight. Flight duration is limited by aircraft endurance rather than crew oxygen supply (Zvezda).

The Yak-130 is equipped with a BTsVM 90-604 onboard digital computer for data processing and exchange of data channeling between integrated systems. Electroautomatics

The Yak-130 cockpit ergonomics are those of a modern glass cockpit combat aircraft with no recourse to electromechanical back-up controls, which are absent (Electroautomatics). The two cockpits are each endowed with three 15.24 cm x 20.32 cm (6 x 8 in) multifunction LED screens. The forward cockpit also features a collimator display (HUD (Heads Up Display)) and a HMTDS (Helmet Mounted Target Designation System). The advanced avionics enhance the Yak-130 ability to conduct the primary advanced training and secondary LCA roles.

At the heart of the Yak-130 data/sensor suite is the K-130.01 complex, which is made up of a number of individual system components. Developed for the Yak-130, the complex K-130.01 oversees and controls the aircraft operations during a number of flight and ground scenarios. In regard to piloting the aircraft, the complex provisions for take-off and landing operations, the outbound and homebound flights, including low-altitude flight operations overland and over sea environments day/night and in fair and adverse weather conditions. The complex also provisions for the integration and functioning of various aircraft equipment by providing a flow-through for data between the complex and various systems, as well as reconfiguration of various equipment in the event of failures (Electroautomatics).

The K-130.01 complex consists of various items of equipment – the BTsVM 90-604 onboard digital computer; MFTSI-0333M colour LED displays (multi-function indicators); HUD-2-02 (ILS-2-02E) indicator (HUD) mounted in front of the windscreen; PUI130 remote control and display, which is installed on the HUD-2-02; PUI130-01 remote control and display, which is independently mounted; BKYTO television and signal switching unit; SWI information input system; NSTS-T HMTDS; KU-31 control button; BSKI-130 synthesising cartographic information unit; LPI-130 information line; BFVI-1; RM-130-1 and RM-130-2 frame mountings (Electroautomatics).

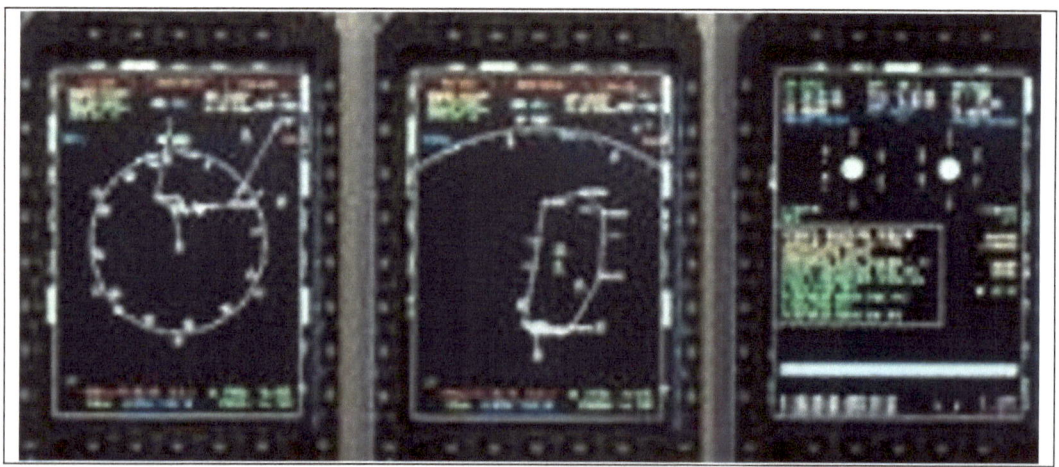

Each of the Yak-130's two cockpits are equipped with three 15.24 cm x 20.32 cm MFTSI-0333M LED colour displays (multi-function indicators) as the major element of crew data display system. The screens can replicate flight, navigation, tactical and other mission specific data such as aircraft systems/stores status. Electroautomatics

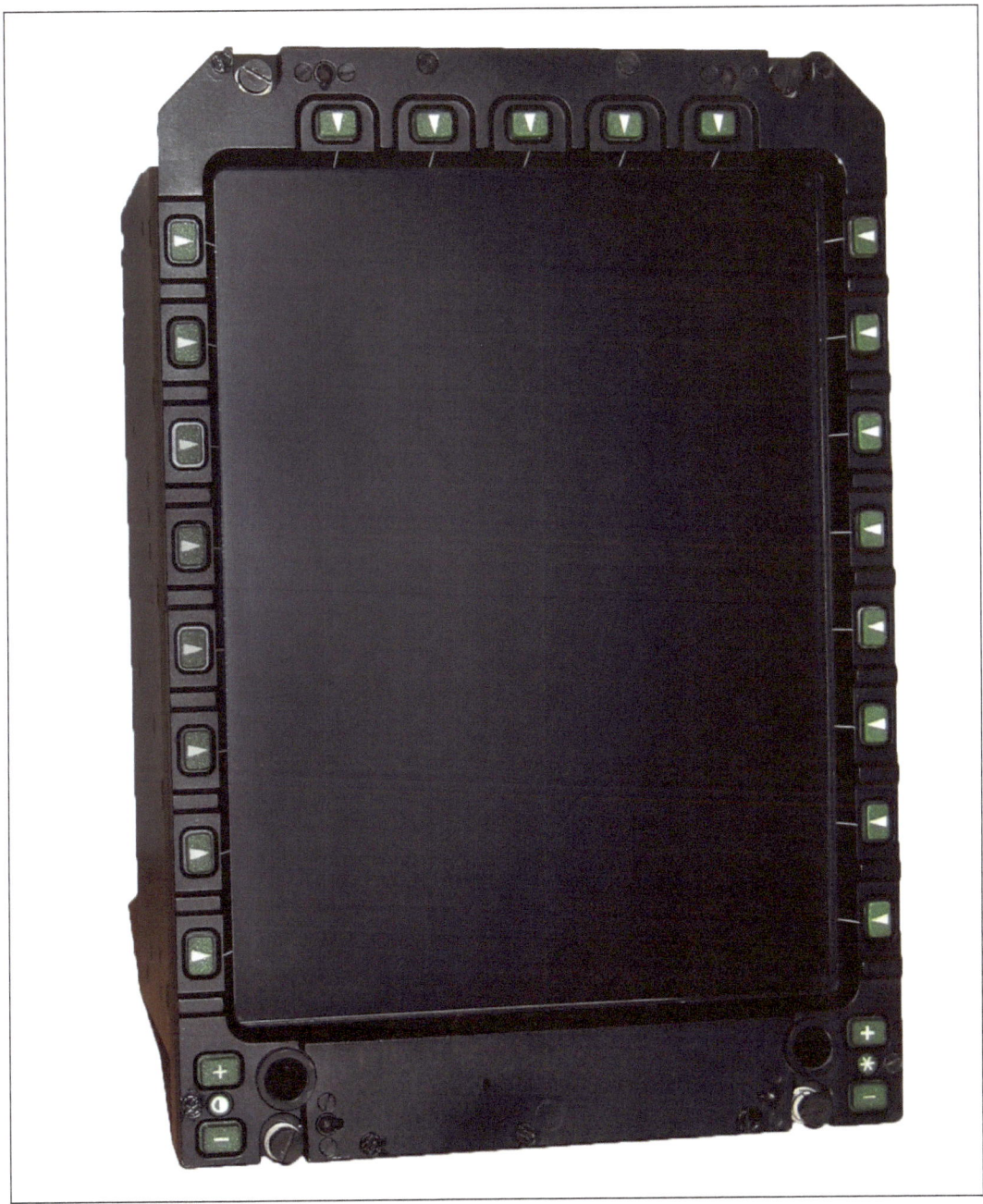

Each of the MFTSI-0333M colour LED displays are equipped with 26 push keys for data/command input. Electroautomatics

The single BTsVM 90-604 onboard digital computer provisions for data processing and exchange of data channeling between integrated systems. While no specific details have been released for the BTsVM 90-604, data released for the 90-604E (export standard) show the system has two computing circuits (VC), television reception/delivery of PC ARINS 429 values are 18 and 8 respectively and reception channels and delivery RK values are 16 and 8 respectively. System power value is equal to 27V – 115V with a power consumption of 100VA for an entire system weight of 15 kg (Electroautomatics).

The six MFTSI-0333M multi-function displays – three in each cockpit – form the major element of the crew data display system. The screens can replicate flight, navigation, tactical and other mission specific data and information of the aircraft systems status, such as engines, fuel, stores, display of warnings and provision of notifications (Electroautomatics).

MFTSI-0333M specification – data furnished by Electroautomatics

Working area: 15.24 x 20.32 cm
Resolution: 768 h1024 pixels
Viewing angles
    Horizontal: 80°
    Vertical: 80°
Number of keys (buttons): 26
Weight: 8 kg
Overall dimensions: 192 x 275 x 208 (units not provided but assumed to be mm)
Interfaces:
    I/O A429 – 12/4
    MKIO
    Television signal
    MKIO
Television signal (RGB) input/output: 1/1

The single HUD-2-02 indicator provides a collimated picture of certain data, such as aircraft status, on a screen at head level. This provisions for easier access of such data to the pilot in the forward cockpit. The complex has a field of view angular diameter of 24 mm and an instantaneous field of view of 17° in the vertical plane and 17° in the horizontal plane when at a standard cockpit distance between pilot eye and HUD (Electroautomatics).

HUD-2-02 specification – data furnished by Electroautomatics

Field of view (FOV), full – diameter: 24°
FOV, instant: 17° x 17° in the vertical and horizontal planes (this conflicts with the 18° x 17° provided in other documentation by the same source)
Weight: 20 kg
Length: 650 mm
Width: 216 mm
Height: 288 mm
Interfaces: I/O A429 – 10/1 - 1/0 RK – 4/1

HUD-2-02 indicator (top) provides a collimated data picture at head level. The PUI130 remote control and display panel (above) is mounted on the HUD-2-02 and controls the various modes for various onboard systems. Electroautomatics

The PUI130 remote control and display panel, mounted on the HUD-2-02, controls the various modes for various onboard systems – RSBN, SINS, SO GO ATC and ARC. Data can be entered automatically or in manual mode through the integral push buttons. The BKYTO television and signal switching unit provisions for switching television signals. The system specified for the export Yak-130 is the BKTSOE with a max input television signal value of 8, a max television output signal RGB value of 6, reception channels/delivery of PC ARINS 429 values of 2 and 1 respectively and three reception channels (Electroautomatics).

The SWI information input system can record and store data of various flight tasking's for further reading. This system has an information volume value for SK-2M of 2 MB, two delivery channels for a single computer and a single reception channel (Electroautomatics).

The NSTS-T/TE HMTS-NE (Helmet Mounted Targeting System-NE) HMTDS provides for targeting through movement of the pilots head through receipt of data obtained by head pointing the sensors – within line of sight. The complex is composed of several components. The DDP-7/T is intended for the 'issue of reference locating device (UL)' to provide collimated images in the field of view of the right eye (Electroautomatics). Two UL units provide for forwarding angular coordinates obtained in the line of sight hemisphere. A TSVM90-607 digital computer facilitates the interaction of systems. The interfacing and data processing of the various NSTS-T/TE components, with each other and with other systems, is overseen by a single TSVM90-607 digital computer. GOST 18977-79 provisions for the discreet transmission/reception of the various signals. NSTS-T/TE line of sight angular coordinates are ± 60° in azimuth and +60° to -15° in elevation (Electroautomatics).

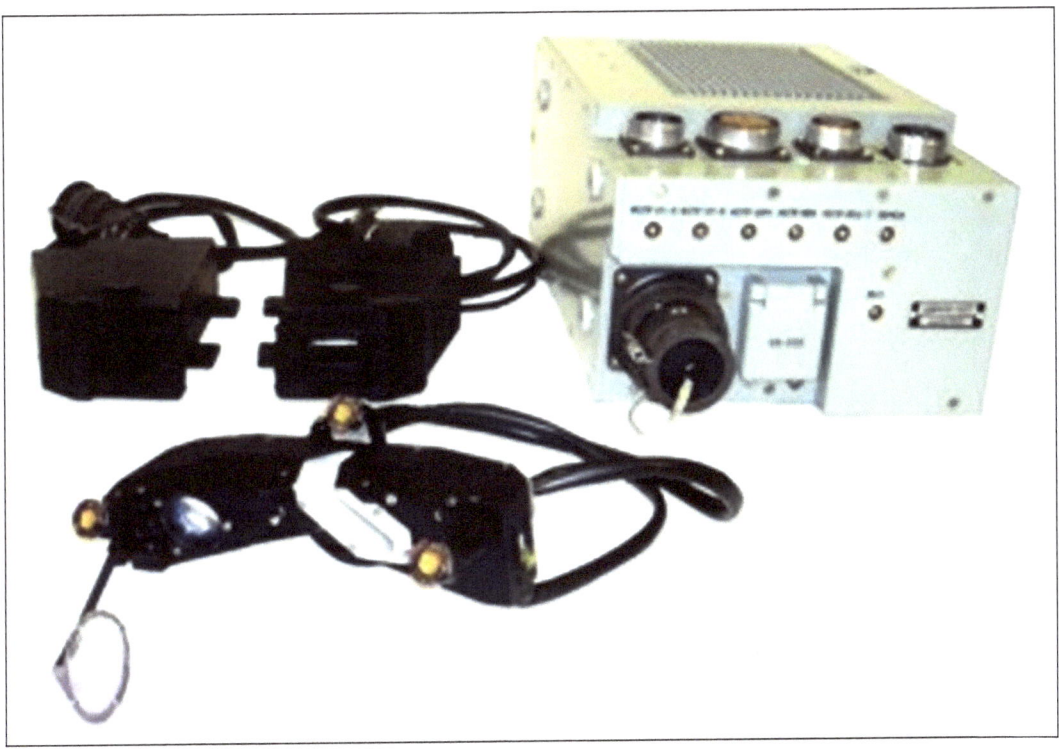

Previous page and this page: The NSTS-T/TE HMTS-NE provides for targeting through data received by head pointing the sensors – within line of sight.
Electroautomatics

NSTS-T specification – data furnished by Electroautomatics

Operating angle
　　Azimuth: ± 60°
　　Elevation: +60° to -15°
Maximum targeting error: 40 angular min
Frequency of updates on information release: 100 Hz
Power consumed by NSTS-T line 115V 400 Hz: not more than 60 VA
Operating temperature range: +44° Centigrade to -40° Centigrade
Weight of NTST-T: 8.4 kg overall
Mean time between failures: 2000 flight hours
Service life: 25 years

The KU-31 control button is utilised for sending electrical control signals 'when you reject buttons along two mutually perpendicular axes by moving the sliders of the potentiometers [which] are mechanically coupled to the button' (Electroautomatics).

BSKI-130 synthesising cartographic information unit. Electroautomatics

The BSKI-130 synthesising cartographic information unit provides for the storing of, reading of, preparation of, conversion of and delivery of the televised picture for the digital map(s) MDTSI. The LPI-130 information line provides for communication of equipment on three channels – MKIO. The BFVI-1; RM-130-1 and RM-130-2 are basically frame mountings for the attachment of equipment blocks (Electroautomatics).

The technical description released for the K-130.01E (export standard) confirms that the integrated digital avionics are built on a MIL-STD-1553B digital data-bus that facilitates high-speed transfer of data between systems (Electroautomatics). While no release of such information has been forthcoming for the K-130-01 equipping domestic Russian Yak-130 aircraft, it is assumed that this will be centred on the MIL-STD-1553B technology incorporated in the K-130.01E.

The Yak-130 is equipped with a plethora of other systems for communications and navigation – can be equipped with BINS-SP-1-SINS (Strap-down Inertial Satellite Navigation System) class, communications complex (Irkut) and is equipped with a KARAT-B-29K-01 airborne system for flight data acquisition (emergency operating system) (Aviaavtomatika).

Russian language Yak-130 graphic showing range, 2100 km; endurance, 3 hours; ceiling, 12500 m; maximum manoeuvre load factor (no external stores), +8/-3 g; maximum controlled angle of attack, ≤35°; resource, 1000 flight hours (30 years); take-off run, 550 m; landing run, 750 m; fuel reserve, suspended fuel tank – 2 x 450 kg and internal fuel, 1700 kg. UAC

The basic Yak-130 advanced trainer design has an empty weight of 4500 kg (MODRF), a normal take-off weight stated as 6350 kg (MODRF) or 5700 kg (Yakovlev), a take-off weight, with full internal fuel load and no external stores, of 7250 kg (Irkut) and a maximum take-off weight of 9000 kg (MODRF & Yakovlev) or 10290 kg (Irkut & UAC). Internal fuel load is stated as 1700 kg (Irkut & UAC) or 1750 kg (Yakovlev). External fuel load is 900 kg, carried in two x PTB-450 external fuel tanks, each with a capacity of 450 kg, which can be carried on the inner wing stations. External stores load is put at 3000 kg, which would include the 900 kg external fuel load.

Extract from Russian language graphic showing various physical and performance characteristics of the Yak-130 – maximum take-off weight, 10290 kg; take-off weight with full fuel load, 7250 kg; maximum external stores load, 3000 kg, nodes of suspension (stores stations ranged from 7-9; maximum true speed (with suspension stores stations), 1060 km/h; maximum vertical velocity, 65 m/s and maximum Mach number, 0.93. UAC

The Yak-130 is credited with an excellent basic flight performance for an aircraft in its class. Maximum level speed is put at 1060 km/h (Irkut and UAC) and 1000 km/h (MODRF), the discrepancy most likely being attributed to whether or not external stores are carried or perhaps a self-imposed restriction for domestic service. The maximum attainable Mach number in level flight is 0.93 (UAC). The design is credited with a maximum vertical velocity of 65 m/s and maximum flight altitude (practical operating ceiling) is 12500 m (Irkut, MODRF, UAC & Yakovlev). Take-off run is put at 550 m, with a landing run value of 750 m (Irkut & UAC). Maximum flight range is put at 1600 km without external fuel or 2100 kg with 2 x PTB-450 external fuel tanks when flying at an altitude of 12000 m (UAC) (MODRF provides a value of 1850 km, without stating with or without external fuel tanks, and Yakovlev states 2000 km on internal fuel). Maximum flight duration with internal and external fuel is put at 3 hours (UAC). In line with meeting the requirement to be capable of emulating the flight characteristics of other aircraft, the Yak-130 is capable of controlled flight at angles of attack of ≤35° (Irkut & Rosoboronexport), <35° (UAC) or <40° (Yakovlev). Maximum manoeuvre load factor, without external stores, is +8/-3 g, with a sustained load factor of 5.2 g when flying at an altitude of 4572 m (UAC).

Yak-130 White 01 (top) and Yak-130 White 02 (bottom). Irkut

Як-130

НОВАЯ КОНЦЕПЦИЯ ОБУЧЕНИЯ

РАНЬШЕ

- Самолет первоначаль-ного обучения
- Учебный самолет для базовой подготовки
- Учебно-боевой двухместный истребитель

С ПОЯВЛЕНИЕМ Як-130

- Самолет первоначального обучения
- Учебно-боевой самолет для основной и повышенной подготовки

Як-130 позволяет отрабатывать все задачи курса обучения, включая применение высокоточного вооружения

Стоимость летного часа Як-130 в 2-5 раз ниже, чем у учебно-боевых истребителей

Russian language graphic with English translation in parenthesis: Як-130 Новая Концепция Обуения (Yak-130 New Concept Trainer (learning), Раньше (Previous generation), Самолет первоначаль-ного обучения (Initial training aircraft), Учебный самолет Для Базовой подготовки (aircraft for basic training), Учебно-Боевой двухнестный истребитель (Military two-seat fighter), С появлением Як-130 (With the advent of the Yak-130), Самолет первоначального обучения (Initial training aircraft), Учебно-боевой самолет для основной и повышенной подготовки (combat training aircraft for primary and advanced training), Як-130 позволяет отрабатывать все задачи курса обучения, включая применение бысокоточного вооружения (Yak-130 allows you to work out all the tasks of the course, including the use of high precision weapons), Стоимость летного часа Як-130 в 2-5 раз ниже, чем у учебно-боевых истребителей (The cost of the flight hour on Yak-130 is 2.5 times lower than that of the combat training fighter). UAC

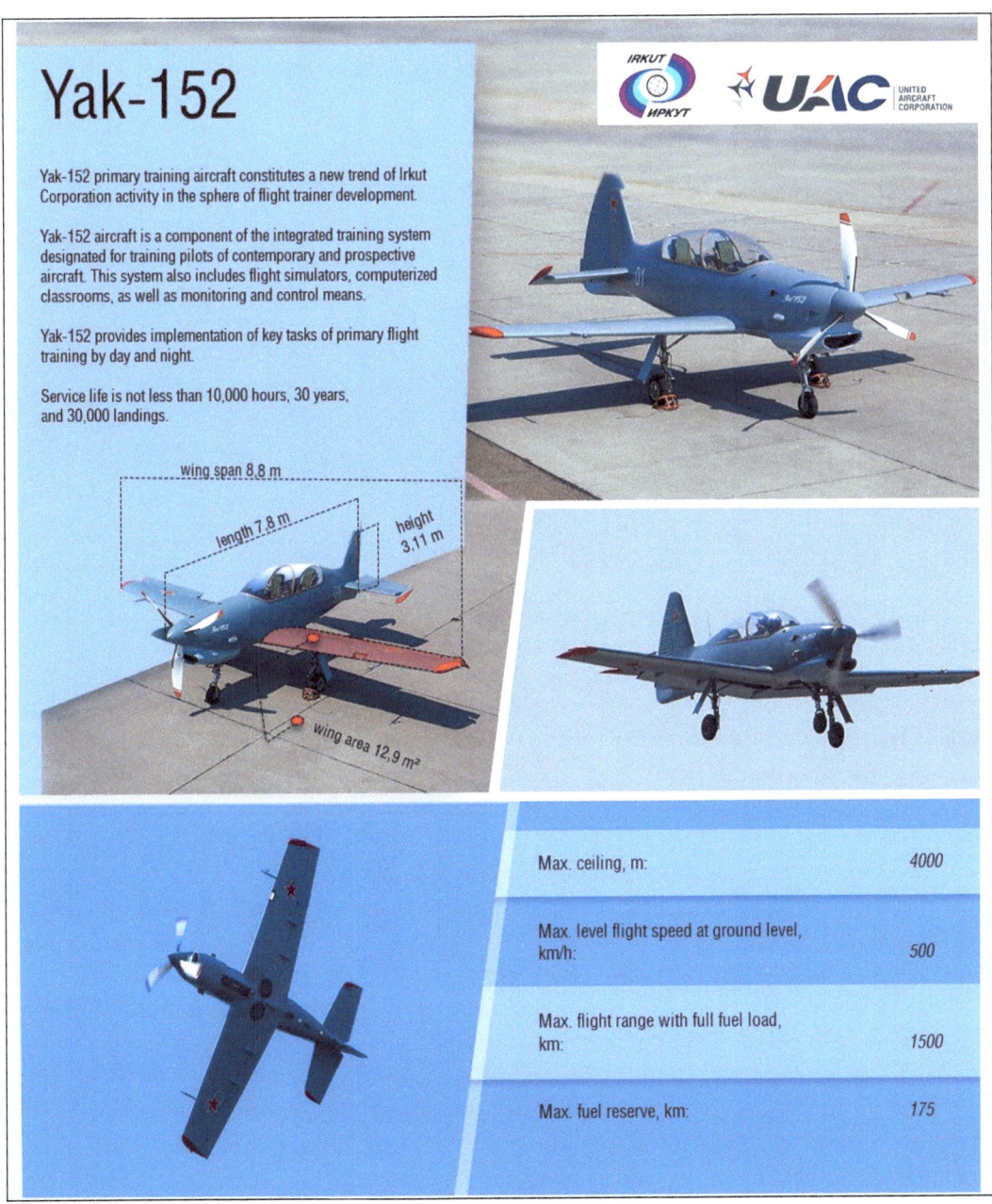

Infographic for the Yak-152 primary training aircraft developed to partner the Yak-130 within the overall training syllabus of the Russian Aerospace Forces/Naval Aviation. UAC

The Yak-130 can be employed as a basic jet training aircraft or an advanced training aircraft, allowing the same platform to be employed in all stages of a pilots jet flight training after advancing from initial training on the Yak-152. The Yak-130 platform can also be employed as a simulator, as well as provisioning real world basic or advanced flight training.

The Yak-130 is destined to replace the Aero Vodochody L-39 in Russian Naval Aviation service, which, in the second decade of the twenty first century, is undergoing a modernisation of its tactical combat aircraft fleets with the introduction of Sukhoi Su-30SM multifunctional strike fighters and RAC MiG-29KR/KUBR shipborne multifunctional strike fighters. Ilyushin

The design of the aircraft/training system allows the Yak-130 to be used for all stages of jet flight training – basic and advanced (Irkut). Before the introduction of the Yak-130 the training syllabus called for prospective pilots to conduct initial pilot training on one platform, basic flying training on another platform and advanced training on yet another platform. The introduction of the Yak-130 allowed for a substantial reduction in aircraft assets required for pilot training. Post Yak-130 introduction the syllabus called for a single platform for initial pilot training and the Yak-130 for basic and advanced flight training (UAC).

The Yak-130 training system provides for the simulation of various flight and operational scenarios, such as air combat training, including the full-spectrum of detection, tracking, weapon cueing/lock-on to target, launch of radar guided and infrared guided air to air missiles, engagement of jamming systems and deployment of defensive countermeasures. The system also provides for simulation of operations with other assets, such as additional aircraft in the formation and airborne (including Beriev A-50U AWACS (Airborne Warning and Control System)) and surface control stations. In the air to surface role, simulations provide for the launch of air to surface ordnance, including radar, television and infrared guided weapons and potentially target engagement with the SNPU-130 pod containing a twin GS-23L 23 mm cannon complex, if fitted. It also provides for simulation of countering surface to air missiles launched at the host aircraft and countering adversary electronic systems through employment of jamming and other defensive aids (Yakovlev).

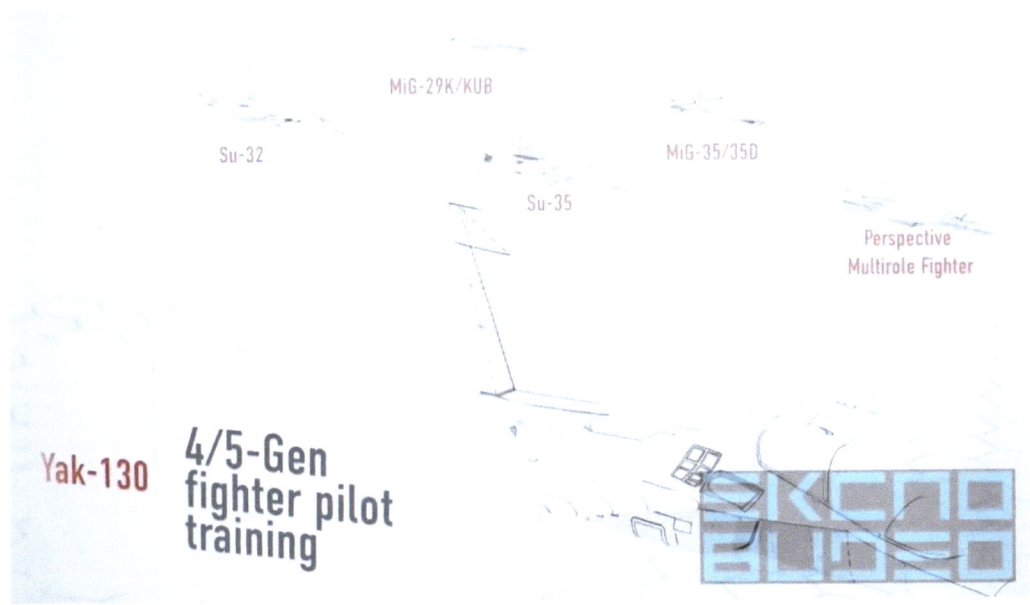

Still graphic depicting the plethora of aircraft types that can be replicated within the Yak-130 training system. Illustrated data is by no means exhaustive. UAC

In the advanced training role the Yak-130 provisions for aircrew to learn the full-spectrum of skills required for moving onto $4^{th}+$, $4^{th}++$ or 5th generation combat aircraft. The Reprogrammiruemaya flight control system enables the Yak-130 to alter the aircraft stability and controllability characteristics in order to replicate those of different aircraft designs to better prepare the flight student for squadron deployment. The overall training complex, of which the Yak-130 is a major element, includes an 'integrated system of objective control, educational computer classes, procedures and specialized aerobatic trainers [Yak-152 planned for the Russian Aerospace Forces]' (Irkut).

The Yak-130 can be used for combat training with the actual employment of weapons against range targets, or can be utilised in a simulation mode for the simulated employment of weapons (Irkut). In the light combat aircraft role the Yak-130 can employ a plethora of guided and unguided air to surface stores and infrared guided air to air missiles of the R-73E and RVV-BD (advanced development of the R-73E) types. As well as disposable munitions, the Yak-130 can be armed with an SNPU-130 container pod containing a GS-23L twin 23 mm cannon, and can be configured with a maximum of two PTB-450 external fuel tanks (each containing 450 kg of fuel) to extend flight range in either training or combat missions (Irkut). Maximum stores load is 3000 kg, carried on nine hard points (domestic Russian Yak-130's operate with eight hard points). In the Light Combat Aircraft role the Yak-130 can be equipped with podded systems for reconnaissance or EW (Electronic Warfare) complexes if required by the operator (UAC). Operational range against a surface target is put at 680 km (Irkut).

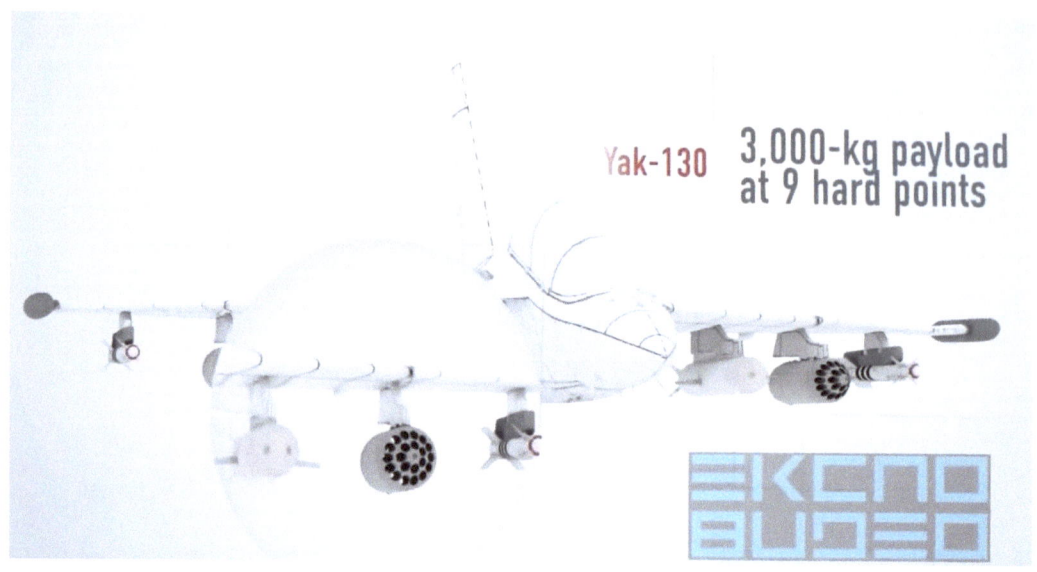

Top: Still graphic detailing the external load carrying ability of the Yak-130 – 3000 kg on 9 stores hard points. The six underwing and two wingtip stations are shown in use, but the fuselage station is shown empty. MODRF documentation shows only eight stores stations are used for domestically operated Yak-130's, the fuselage station being omitted. Above: Belarus Air Force Yak-130 armed with a SNPU-130 container pod containing a GS-23L twin 23 mm cannon complex on the fuselage station and a B13L pod, containing 5 x 122 mm S-13T unguided rockets, on the starboard inboard station. UAC/Irkut

Specified bomb/rocket/missile armament options include 50, 100, 250 and 500 kg class unguided bombs, KAB-500Kr television guided bombs, S-8, S-13 or S-25 rockets and R-73E infrared guided air to air missiles (Irkut). The Aircraft can also, at operator request, be configured with battlefield guided air to surface missiles, such as Kh-29 class missiles, with the Raytheon AGM-65 Maverick class weapon specified as a potential export customer option (Irkut & MODRF). Additional weapon options can be cleared through the open architecture avionics.

The Yak-130 can be configured with a maximum of four R-73E infrared guided air to air missiles – two carried on the outer wing stations (top) and two carried on the wingtip stations (above). Rostec/Irkut

The only guided air to air missile specified for the Yak-130 is the GosMKB Vympel (TMC) R-73E infrared homing missile, a maximum of four of which can be carried, two on each of the outer and wingtip stations. The R-73E was a generation ahead of its rivals when it entered service in the 1980's, comparable systems being fielded by NATO (North Atlantic Treaty Organisation) air arms only in the first decade of the twenty first century. The R-73 was developed with high agility as a design driver, augmented by the ability of the pilot of the host aircraft, be it an Su-27 or MiG-29 derivative, to cue the weapon to a target at up to 60° off-boresight via the HPS (Helmet Pointing System) or the twenty first century helmet mounted target designation system – NSTS-T/TE in the Yak-130. A High level of manoeuvrability was achieved through a combination of a number of design traits – four forward control fins, elevators attached to the rear fins, which are fixed, and deflector vanes positioned in the nozzle of the rocket engine (TMC).

The R-73E, which is carried on and launched from Aviation Trigger P-72-1D series launchers, has a length of 2.9 m; diameter, 0.17 m; wing span, 0.51 m and a control plane span of 0.38 m, launch weight being 105 kg. The missile, which has a longer reach than most western equivalents, has a maximum engagement range of 30 km against a head-on target and a minimum engagement range of 0.3 km against a tail-on target manoeuvring at up to 12 g. The missile can be launched at altitudes from 0.02 up to 20 km, the all-aspect passive infrared seeker head guiding the missile to the target, which would be destroyed by the integral 8 kg expanding rod warhead (TMC).

This Russian Aerospace Forces Yak-130 is configured with R-73E missiles on the outboard wing stations, B8M1 rocket pods on the intermediate wing stations and B13L rocket pods on the inner wing stations. Irkut

Guided air to surface weapons in the class of the Kh-29 short-range battlefield missile could be carried by the Yak-130, but this weapon is not a standard option as of 2019. In the Belarussian Air Force the Yak-130 has a ground attack role that was previously the preserve of the Su-25 ground attack aircraft. The primary guided air to surface armament in Belarussian service is the KAB-500Kr guided bomb unit, which weighs 520 kg. The KAB-500 weapons are 3.05 m in length with a 0.35 m diameter and can be released from altitudes of 0.5 to 5 km at carrier speeds of 550 to 1100 km/h. Specified accuracy/root mean square deviation is 4-7 m, the target being destroyed by the 380 kg concrete piercing high explosive penetrator warhead in the KAB-500Kr (TMC).

The S-80KOM/Ts-8BM unguided rocket, carried in B8M1 rocket pods, each of which contain twenty rockets, can be launched singly or in salvo fire under environmental conditions of ambient temperatures ±60° Centigrade. The B8M1 rocket pod, which can be carried on the inner and intermediate wing stations, can be substituted with the B13L pod containing 5 x 122 mm S-13T unguided rockets, a maximum of 20 of which could be carried, five in each of four pods. Like the B8M1 pod, the B13L can launch its rockets singly or in salvo under the same environmental operating conditions. The B8M1 and B13L are carried on BD3-USK-B beam holders (Vympel). The standard unguided bomb options can include OFAB-100-120 general purpose bombs and FAB-250 (OFAB-250-270) general purpose bombs.

The PTB-450 external fuel tanks are an integral element of the Yak-130 external stores options, increasing training flight endurance and facilitating ease of transfer between air bases in Russia's vast expanse. Irkut

As noted above, other than armaments, other stores options for the Yak-130 include the ability to carry two PTB-450 external fuel tanks on the inner wing stations, electronic warfare pods on the wingtip stations (this would reduce to two the number of R-73E missiles that could be accommodated) and, depending on operator requirements, a podded airborne reconnaissance system. The Yak-130 can also be equipped with a suite of two REB containers for ejection of decoy clutter to protect against guided missiles attacks.

The Yak-130 can be equipped with electronic warfare pods on the wingtip stations (type would depend on customer requirement). While the electronic warfare suite would be applicable to the LCA role, the disposable infrared decoy flares pertain to the training and LCA roles. UAC

Yak-130 – data furnished by Irkut, UAC, Yakovlev, MODRF & Rosoboronexport

Length: 11.49 m
Height: 4.76 m
Wingspan: 9.84 m with wingtip stores (Irkut, UAC & Rosoboronexport) and 9.72 m without wingtip stores (MODRF)
Wing area: 23.52 m^2 (Irkut & UAC)
The base chassis: 3.945 m (Irkut)
Track chassis: 2.53 m (Irkut, UAC & Yakovlev)
Empty weight: 4500 kg (MODRF)
Normal weight: 6350 kg (MODRF) or 5700 kg (Yakovlev)
Take-off weight with full internal fuel load and no external stores: 7250 kg (Irkut & UAC)
Maximum take-off weight: 10290 kg (Irkut, UAC & Rosoboronexport) or 9000 kg (MODRF & Yakovlev)
Internal fuel load: 1700 kg (Irkut & UAC)
External fuel load: 900 kg in 2 x 450 kg PTB-450 fuel tanks
Powerplant: 2 x non-afterburning AI-225-25 turbofan engines, each rated at 2500 kgf thrust
Maximum speed, level flight: 1060 km/h (Irkut & UAC or 1000 km/h (MODRF)
Maximum Mach number: 0.93
Maximum vertical velocity (climb) rate: 65 m/s
Maximum flight altitude (practical ceiling): 12500 m (Irkut, MODRF, UAC & Yakovlev)
Maximum flight angles of attack: ≤35° (Irkut, UAC & Rosoboronexport) or <40° (Yakovlev)
Take-off run: 550 m (Irkut & UAC)
Landing run: 750 m (Irkut & UAC)
Maximum range: 1600 km without external fuel or 2100 kg with two PTB-450 external fuel tanks at 12000 m flight altitude (Irkut & UAC). MODRF states 1850 km, without stating with or without external fuel tanks. Yakovlev states 2000 km on internal fuel
Maximum flight duration with internal and external fuel: 3 hours
Maximum manoeuvre load factor without external stores): +8/-3 g
Sustained maneuver load factor at 4572 m flight altitude: 5.2 g
Maximum stores load: 3000 kg
Number of stores stations: 9 (MODRF states 8 for domestically operated aircraft)
Armament: unguided rockets and bombs of various calibres/weights, R-73E infrared guided air to air missiles, KAB-500Kr 500 kg guided bomb unit, SNPU-130 pod containing GS-23L twin 23 mm cannon complex on the fuselage station and PU NUR podded systems for reconnaissance or electronic warfare complexes and battlefield guided air to surface missiles (Kh-29 class (option))
Crew: 2
Service life: 1000 hours, equating to 30 years of service

ЯК-130

Page 52: A Yak-130 fuselage is moved into the final assembly line. Page 53-54: Yak-130's during final assembly at Irkutsk Aviation Plant. Irkut

Yak-130 White 134. Irkut

The major customer for the Yak-130 is the Russian Federation, with 109 aircraft delivered by October 2018. The Yak-130 design had completed Preliminary State Joint Tests in November 2007. This involved Yak-130 01 in flight performance and characteristics testing with dedicated engine testing being allocated to Yak-130 02. Completion of this phase was a milestone on the road to implementation of full series production (UAC). A new stage of testing commenced on 16 September 2008 at the 929th State Air Test Centre, GLITs them, V.P. Chkalov, with the arrival of Yak-130 01 and 02. The initial stage of State Joint Tests of the Yak-130, configured with armament, was completed in April 2009. The armament options were expanded for the next phase of testing, which was completed in December 2009, marking the completion of the overall State Joint Testing, which paved the way for the Yak-130 entry into service (UAC).

The first contract for the production of a batch of serial Yak-130 for the Russian Air Force had been signed in early 2006, the twelve aircraft to be delivered in 2006 (4), 2007 (4) and 2008 (4). This ambitious schedule would be subject to alterations as the delivery process was slowed and the contract extended into 2010. Production of the twelve Yak-130's commenced at the Sokol Aviation Plant in 2008, with the last completed in 2010, the first of the twelve aircraft having conducted its maiden flight on 19 May 2009. Pilot and ground engineers underwent training on the Yak-130 at the Lipetsk aviation training centre during 2009 and the aircraft began entering Russian air force service in February 2010 (UAC).

In 2006 the Irkutsk Aviation Plant (JSC Irkut Corporation) had been brought into the program, this eventually becoming the centre of serial production for domestic and export aircraft beyond the initial batch of twelve serial production aircraft built at the Sokol Aviation Plant. The Ministry of Defence of the Russian Federation ordered an extended batch of 55 Yak-130, the first aircraft being delivered form this contract in 2010. By 2015, the year the Russian Federation Air Force was absorbed into the Russian Aerospace Forces, the Yak-130 was firmly established in service, training aircrew for the new generation of tactical combat aircraft then being similarly established in Russian service. Shortly after the Aerospace Forces was established in August 2015, a batch of four Yak-130's were delivered to the 200th training aviation base, Armavir aviation training base – early October 2015. These aircraft would enter service with the Krasnodar High Military Aviation School. The transfer flights distanced around 5500 km from Irkut to the Krasnodar Krai, requiring three intermediate stopovers for refuelling at the air bases at Novosibirsk, Chelyabinsk and Borisoglebsk (MODRF). Some of the transfer flights were conducted in adverse weather conditions of precipitation, dense cloud, high side winds, with ground temperatures, at the time of Irkut departure, of minus 30° Centigrade below zero. It was determined that the Yak-130 performed extremely well in such conditions. Further deliveries continued to Armavir Aviation training base, for service with the Krasnodar flight school, through December 2016 (MODRF) – this was the year that the Yak-130 design set world records for various climb to heights in clean configuration and with external payloads for a Jet powered aircraft with a take-off weight class of 6000-9000 kg (TsAGI).

Quartet of Russian Aerospace Forces Yak-130. Irkut

Yak-130 White 134 (top) and Russian Federation Aerospace Forces Yak-130's White 27 and 28 (above). Irkut

Vertical tails of a trio of Russian Aerospace Forces Yak-130's, White 44, 34 and 36. Irkut

The Yak-130 was selected as the platform for two Russian Federation aerobatic display teams – Stinzhi, which conducted initial flights on the Yak-130 at Borisoglebsk training centre circa 17 March 2015, and Wings of Tavrida, which conducted its first public display at MAKS-2015 (MODRF).

YAK-130

The Yak-130 is overall heavier than the L-39 in Russian Air Force/Aerospace Forces service, 4500 kg & 3580 kg respectively for empty weight and 10290 kg (9000 kg) and 5670 kg respectively for maximum take-off weight. There was not much between the designs in regard to range, but the Yak-130 had a maximum operating speed in the region of 300 km/h in excess of its predecessor. In overall design, the Yak-130 is a generation and a half, if not two generations, ahead of the L-39. In this regard it would be unwise to compare the capabilities of both designs as they were designed in different eras for the requirements of their respective times.

Previous page and this page: As well as operational training schools the Yak-130 is operated by trials organisations and on developer trials. Yak-130's White 02 (top) and White 01 (bottom) are shown. Irkut

YAK-130

Yak-130's Red 71, with spine mounted air brake deployed (top) and Red 72 (above) of the Republic of Belarus Air Force. Irkut

Belarus operates her small fleet of Yak-130 in a dual capacity as advanced jet training aircraft and as light combat aircraft, armed with guided and unguided air to air and air to surface weapons. Irkut

The Yak-30 has gained orders from a number of export customers, Algeria, Bangladesh, Belarus Laos and Myanmar. The first deployment outside the Russian Federation took place when Yak-130 02 was dispatched to Malaysia in late 2005 for a defense exhibition at the commencement of the export drive (UAC). The initial details of a contract to deliver sixteen Yak-130UBS aircraft to Algeria was signed in 2006 and the first of these aircraft conducted its maiden flight from the Irkutsk Aviation Plant on 21 August 2009 (pilots, Roman Taskaev and Sergey Mikhaylyuk). The first export aircraft were delivered in 2011 (UAC).

Other than the initial order for sixteen aircraft by Algeria, open source government information suggests Bangladesh ordered sixteen Yak-130 aircraft, Laos ordered sixteen – the first being delivered to that nation on 20 December 2018 and transferred to Vientiane airbase, Laos capital in January 2019 – Myanmar ordered sixteen Yak-130 in two batches of 10 and 6, the second batch being delivered circa 26 March 2019 and Belarus ordered twelve.

Belarus, which is a CSTO (Collective Security Treaty Organisation) party, along with the Russian Federation, ordered the first four Yak-130 aircraft on 18 December 2012 as part of the overall treaty on development of military cooperation between Belarus and the Russian Federation, singed on 10 December 2009. The four Yak-130 were delivered to the 116th Guard Attack Aviation Base, Lida, Republic of Belarus, on 15 April 2015. The aircraft were transported from Irkut to Lida aboard Ilyushin

Il-76 transport aircraft for assembly by Irkut engineers before hand over to the Belarus Air Force on 27 April 2015. A further batch of four Yak-130 was delivered to Belarus military unit 19764 at Lida on 23 November 2016 and the final batch of Yak-130, from the twelve ordered, was delivered on 11 May 2019 (MODRB).

The LCA role, armed with guided and unguided weapons, has taken on some significance for the Yak-130 in the Belarus Air Force, which operates it alongside the Su-25SM ground attack aircraft. For the air to air role the Belarus Yak-30 is armed with the R-73E infrared guided air to air missile – Lida based Yak-130's conducted launches of R-73E missiles on 4 and 5 February 2016 – and the KAB-500Kr guided bomb unit is employed in the ground attack role alongside unguided weapons referred to above. Belarus began testing KAB-500Kr guided bomb units in August 2015 (MODRB).

Belarus personnel were trained on the Yak-130 at the Centre for the Organisation of Aviation Personnel Training at Zhukovsky, Russia (MODRB). As the light combat aircraft role took on prominence amid a NATO buildup in the Baltic States, Belarus Yak-130's conducted nighttime landings on sections of highway from 17-19 May 2016 (MODRB) as off-base operations were adopted to enable missions to be conducted even if the airbase is heavily damaged – Lida being located a mere 40 or so km from the Lithuanian border. Combat training was conducted from 2017 at Ashuluk training range in the Russian Federation and Belarus Yak-130's came second in the Attack Aviation category of the Aviadarts element of the Russian Army-2018 games, open to international competitors. The Yak-130's were competing against units equipped with Su-25 and Su-25SM (modernised) attack aircraft (MODRF).

A Belarus Yak-130 arrives in Russia for the Aviadarts tactical competition on 27 July 2019. MODRF

Top: A Yak-130, silhouetted against a picturesque sky, configured with R-73E missiles, PTB-450 external fuel tanks and unidentified stores on the intermediate wing stations. Above: Yak-130 White 01 has been the mainstay of development of the Yak-130 light combat aircraft capability. The aircraft is configured with R-73 missiles on the wingtip stations, B8M1 rocket pods on the intermediate wing stations and external fuel tanks on the inner wing stations. Irkut

Top: Light Combat Aircraft variants of the Yakovlev Yak-130 emerged in the 1990's. This model of a radar equipped LCA Yak-130 derivative dates back to 2000/2001. The aircraft is configured for the air combat mission with R-73E infrared guided air to air missiles on the wingtip and outboard wing stations, RVV AE active radar guided medium range air to air missiles on the intermediate wing stations, external fuel tanks on the inner wing stations and a SNPU-130 container pod containing a twin GS-23L cannon on the fuselage station. Above: A 2014 graphic depicting the Yak-130 configured with what appears to be representative of radar guided air to surface missile on the inner wing stations Author/UAC

As of mid-2019, the LCA role is very much a secondary one in the Russian Federation, but is utilised more with Yak-130 export operators. Future developments may focus mainly on the LCA capability, including provisioning for the ability to refuel in-flight (Irkut), which may take the form of a fixed in-flight refueling probe in a similar manner to that developed for the Yak-130s western European sibling, the M-346. Such a capability is not currently a Russian Aerospace Forces/Russian Naval Aviation requirement within the advanced training role syllabus. A demonstration in-flight refueling probe may be installed in a trials aircraft if such a requirement is identified for a customer.

Mock-up of the M-346, showing the fixed in-flight refueling probe installation on the starboard forward fuselage. Author

The LCA capability can be enhanced through the addition of an opto-electronic complex that would facilitate the ability to conduct all-weather operations day/night (Irkut). A radar complex (unspecified) is an option that would transform the Yak-130 into a truly multifunctional strike fighter able to operate with radar guided missiles for air to air (RVV-AE) and air to surface roles, extending the distances that targets can be engaged at out to well beyond visual range (Irkut). While there is sparse data on a potential radar equipped Yak-130 development available, Irkut confirms that Yak-130 White 01 has been utilised as a test platform for demonstrating an electro-optical station, which would vastly increase the Yak-130's combat potential and the ability to further expand the syllabus of the advanced training role.

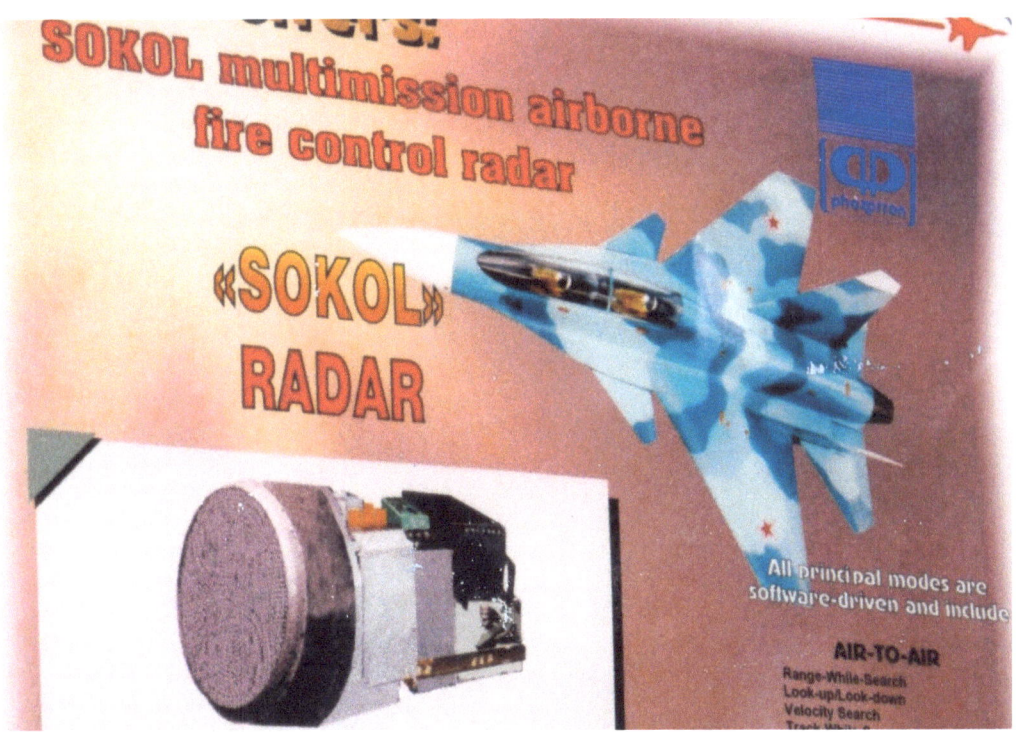

Top (Primary sensor for a notional Russian LCA in the late 1990's and into the 2000's was the Sokol X-band multi-functional fire control radar, credited with an air target detection range of ~180 km in the forward hemisphere and ~80 km in the rear hemisphere. Above: This Yak-130 model, configured as a LCA, was presented at trade expositions in the second decade of the twenty first century. Author/UAC

Yak-130 White 01. Irkut

Yak-130 White 01 has been employed in various weapon trial configurations enhancing the Yak-130 LCA capability. Irkut

The AI-222-25F (AI-322/F), which powers the CATIC L-15A Advanced Fighter Trainer, is specified for the unbuilt Yak-135 LCA, allowing such platforms to operate at speeds up to Mach 1.6 (Ivchenko-Progress). The Yak-135 would retain the high level of maneuverability of the Yak-130 through the incorporation of 'gas-dynamic stability of the engine' building on experience gained on the Yak-130 powered by the AI-222-25. The AI-222-25F incorporates a FADEC (Full Authority Digital Engine

Control) complex. A multi-range of engine performance levels and engine diagnostics can be attained, overseen by a multi-channel automatic control system. A thrust vector control complex can be incorporated for the engine exhaust nozzle (Ivchenko-Progress). This would be developed to meet a specific customer requirement should this arise.

AI-322F (AI-222-25F) – data furnished by Ivchenko-Progress & Motor Sich

Length: 3070 mm
Full diameter: 880 mm
Height: 1084 mm
Length: 2238 mm
Weight, dry: 560 kg
Full afterburner power (S/L static, ISA)
Maximum thrust: 4500 kgf
Specific fuel consumption: 1.9 kg/h/kgf
Full afterburner power (Height=11000 m; Mach=1.4; *inlet = 0.97; ISA)
Thrust: 2760 kgf
Specific fuel consumption: 0.66 kg/h/kgf

The unbuilt Yak-135 LCA derivative of the Yak-130 advanced trainer is specified to be powered by the AI-322F (AI-222-25F). Ivchenko-Progress

Top: The CATIC L-15A AFT is powered by the AI-222-25F (AI-322F) afterburning turbofan engine specified for the unbuilt Yak-135. Above: Whilst the Yak-135 remains, in 2019, an unrealised design concept, the Yak-130, Red 62 here at Armavir training base circa 2016, has established itself in domestic Russian service as an advanced training aircraft with a significant secondary LCA capability. CATIC/MODRF

Approaching the third decade of the twenty first century the Yak-130 is firmly established in service as an advanced trainer with a significant secondary air to air and air to surface capability. Regardless of whether or not a dedicated LCA variant is developed, the existing design will undergo capability updates to enhance combat capability to meet end user requirements.

In the Russian Federation Aerospace Forces, the Yak-130 (bottom) is established in service where it will, under 2019 planning, partner the Yak-152 (top) in the overall aviation training syllabus. UAC

GLOSSARY

APU	Auxiliary Power Unit
AWACS	Airborne Warning and Control System
CATIC	China National Aero-Technology Import & Export Corporation
cm	Centimetre
CSTO	Collective Security Treaty Organisation
EES	Emergency Escape System
EW	Electronic Warfare
FADEC	Full Authority Digital Engine Control
FBW	Fly-By-Wire
FCS	Flight Control System
g	Gravity (1 g = 1 x Earth gravity)
HMTDS	Helmet Mounted Target Designation System
HMTS	Helmet Mounted Targeting System
HP	High Pressure
HPS	Helmet Pointing System
HUD	Heads Up Display
in	Inch
kg	Kilogram
kgf	Kilogram force
kg/h/kgf	Kilogram per hour per kilogram force
km	Kilometre
km/h	Kilometres per hour
kN	Kilo Newton
kg/s	Kilogram per second
lb.	Pound, unit of weight
LP	Low Pressure
m	Metre
m^2	Metre squared
Mach	1 Mach = the speed of sound (this varies with altitude)
MB	Megabyte
MiG	Mikoyan
mm	Millimetre
MODRB	Ministry of Defence of the Republic of Belarus
MODRF	Ministry of Defence of the Russian Federation
NATO	North Atlantic Treaty Organisation
RAC	Russian Aircraft Corporation
SINS	Strapdown Inertial Navigation System
Su	Sukhoi
TMC	Tactical Missiles Corporation
TsAGI	Central Aerodynamic Institute
USSR	Union of Soviet Socialist Republics
V	Volts

x	Multiplication
±	Plus or minus
~	Approximately equal to (can also be used to mean asymptotically equal)
°	Degree(s)
≤	Less than or equal to
<	Less than

ABOUT THE AUTHOR

Hugh Harkins FRAS is a historian and author with an extensive research background in astro/geophysics and studies/research in the wider scientific, aeronautic, astronautic and nautical technical and historical fields. He is also involved in research in the field of Scottish history, which formed a significant element of an otherwise scientific undergraduate degree. Hugh has published in excess of sixty books; non-fiction and fiction, writing under his given name as well as utilising several pseudonyms. He has also written for several international magazines, whilst his work has been used as reference for many other projects ranging from the aviation industry, international news corporations and film media to encyclopaedias, museum exhibits and the computer gaming industry. Hugh is a member of the Institute of Physics and is an elected Fellow of the Royal Astronomical Society. He currently resides in his native Scotland. Other titles by the author include:

Russia's Coastal Missile Shield - Bal-E & Bastion Mobile Coastal Cruise Missile Complexes
Iskander - Mobile Tactical Aero-Ballistic/Cruise Missile Complex
Orbital/Fractional Orbit Bombardment System - The Soviet Globalnaya Raketa
Counter-Space Defence Co-Orbital Satellite Fighter
Russia's Strategic Missile Carrier/Bomber Roadmap 2018-2040 – PAK DA, Tu-160M2, Tu-95MSM & Tu-22M3M
Sukhoi T-50/PAK FA - Russia's 5th Generation 'Stealth' Fighter
Sukhoi Su-35S 'Flanker' E - Russia's 4++ Generation Super-Manoeuvrability Fighter
Sukhoi Su-34 'Fullback'
Sukhoi Su-30MKK/MK2/M2 - Russo Kitashiy Striker from Amur
Soviet Mixed Power Experimental Fighter Aircraft – Piston-Liquid Propellant Rocket Engine/Piston-Ramjet/Piston-Pulsejet & Piston-Compressor Jet Engine Designs of the 1940's
MiG-35/D 'Fulcrum' F – Towards the Fifth Generation
Air War over Syria, Tu-160, Tu-95MS & Tu-22M3 - Cruise Missile and Bombing Strikes on Syria, November 2015-February 2016
Sukhoi Su-27SM(3)/SKM
Russian/Soviet Aircraft Carrier & Carrier Aviation Design & Evolution Volume 1 - Seaplane Carriers, Project 71/72, Graf Zeppelin, Project 1123 ASW Cruiser & Project 1143-1143.4 Heavy Aircraft Carrying Cruiser
Light Battle Cruisers and the Second Battle of Heligoland Bight
British Battlecruisers of World War 1 - Operational Log, July 1914-June 1915
Eurofighter Typhoon - Storm over Europe
North American F-108 Rapier - Mach 3 Interceptor
Convair YB-60 - Fort Worth Overcast
Boeing X-36 Tailless Agility Flight Research Aircraft
X-32 - The Boeing Joint Strike Fighter
X-35 - Progenitor to the F-35 Lightning II
X-45 Uninhabited Combat Air Vehicle
Into The Cauldron - The Lancaster MK.I Daylight Raid on Augsburg
Hurricane IIB Combat Log - 151 Wing RAF, North Russia 1941
RAF Meteor Jet Fighters in World War II, an Operational Log
Typhoon IA/B Combat Log - Operation Jubilee, August 1942
Defiant MK.I Combat Log - Fighter Command, May-September 1940
Blenheim MK.IF Combat Log - Fighter Command Day Fighter Sweeps/Night Interceptions, September 1939 - June 1940
Fortress MK.I Combat Log - Bomber Command High Altitude Bombing Operations, July-September 1941

www.ingramcontent.com/pod-product-compliance
Lightning Source LLC
Chambersburg PA
CBHW042012150426
43195CB00003B/100